MW00827102

Seltzer's Rainbow Heart

written by
Jayne DiGregorio

illustrated by
Kirsty McAlpine

IN GRATITUDE: My Rock & Roll boy who loved our Seltzer so dearly.
My beautiful family & friends for all your love & support; Kirsty for bringing my words to life through her magical gift; MaryAnne for her positive vibes & editing; specail shoutout to Giada for her extra set of eyes. Stefanie for keeping me on course & my Boo Bear.

Special Paws up to all the beautiful animals in the world (Truffle, Izzy, Jules, Coco)
Remembering Major, Tosca, Duce, Diva, Meecho, Patches, Puccini, Perla, Queenie, Lady, Fletcher.

I carry your heart , I carry your heart in mine. Mia Pia/Poparoo

POPPY DREAMZ
Copyright ©2018 JAYNE DiGREGORiO
All rights reserved.

Dedicated to my little Seltzer
A story about everlasting Love.

Once upon a time,
in early December.

A Yorkie was born
with a name you'll remember.

The littlest dog
with a rainbow heart so true.

Little Seltzer, little Seltzer,
how do you do?

A rainbow heart,
a rainbow heart?

I never heard
of a rainbow heart.

Yes, it's true,
a rainbow heart.

Seltzer the Yorkie
has a rainbow heart.

Her rainbow heart
is so full of love,

The kind, like in movies
that you always hear of.

Warm and fuzzy
with lots of smiles,

Everyone knew Seltzer
from miles & miles.

Seltzer has big,
bright sparkly eyes,

And plays all day
under the baby blue skies.

She gives doggie kisses
that are sugary sweet,

Laughing with friends
and strangers she would meet.

Her rainbow heart
had the prettiest colors.

Like a red cherry pie,
sweet like no other.

Splashed with orange,
yellow, and glowed like the sun.

Seltzer's heart was so happy,
a great ball of fun!

Her heart sparkled green,
like a neon firefly.

Glittering indigo
and blue like the sky.

Sprinkles of violet,
shined in her brave heart,

All the colors of the rainbow
set Seltzer apart.

Seltzer gave her love
that she had inside.

Love is for sharing,
not something to hide.

Seltzer loved everyone,
no matter size or color.

That's what made her
a dog like no other.

But one day when Seltzer
walked into the room;
Something felt different,
A feeling of gloom.

The sparkle in Seltzer's eyes was gone.
Like the sun when it hides
from a gloomy storm.

Her big rainbow heart
changed colors too;
Shades of gray filled the sky,
that were once blue.

She tried to smile as she walked on by,
Weak and frail, she still held her head up high.

"I love you my friends, so don't be sad,
I heard Doggie Heaven isn't that bad.
It's just a new place for me to go,
So my rainbow heart can once again glow."

Everyone hugged her and tried not to cry,
One last doggie kiss, one last goodbye.
Her little tail wagged, out the door she went,
She turned one last time to look at her friends.

The next day friends waited;
and the next day, the same,
Waiting for Seltzer,
but nobody came.

They looked at each other
with sad puppy dog eyes,
It started to rain,
just like tears from the skies.

"I'm so mad, I just want to scream!"
Shouted Bear Boo. "This must be a bad dream!"

"I miss Seltzer so much, it's just not fair,
I'm going to be bad; I really don't care."

"Don't be that way," said Princess Yum Yum
"Being bad is just really dum dum!"

"Let's remember all the great times
with Seltzer in the park,
Catching frisbees and balls,
and running 'til dark."

"Oh yes! Of course!"
Bear Boo nodded and smiled.
As all of her friends gathered around
"Remember how Seltzer would prance when she ran,
Singing, "Catch me, catch me, catch me if you can?"

Remember the winters?
She would jump in the snow!
We would all chase the snowballs
in zero below.

Inside we would laugh;
ate 'til our bellies got fat.
"Oh, now I'm hungry,"
said Princess Yum Yum the cat.

Major the Shepherd
Stood tall in his glory;
Barked so loud,
to get attention for his story.

"I love how Seltzer
thought she was as BIG as me,
Our little protector
She wouldn't hurt a flea!"

Cheech suddenly remembered,
"She would steal all my sticks!
But I didn't care, because
she loved all my tricks!"

Seltzer's happiness shined
like the sun in the sky,
That's why it was so hard
To say good-bye.

Suddenly,
right before their eyes;

Something magical happened,
much to their surprise.

Fun memories of Seltzer filled the room,
With color after color, like flowers in bloom.

The rainbow heart of Seltzer
appeared so bright,
And everyone realized something
important that night.

Even though Seltzer was
in Doggie Heaven afar;
Her rainbow heart shined
like a big bright star.

She led by example,
with unconditional love so true.
We can all be like Seltzer
and have rainbow hearts too!

~ The End ~

Made in the USA
Las Vegas, NV
03 December 2022

60279407R00024